I TOLD THE STARS ABOUT YOU

BE MY MOON

ISHA KANSAL

Copyright © Isha Kansal
All Rights Reserved.

Dedicated to all the people who believe in love

Contents

Contents

Contents

Contents

Contents

Contents

Contents

Prologue

THANKYOU, for believing in me and purchasing this book. To potray all the emotions, my heart and soul experienced, in these past few days, I had to undergo a journey marked by believing, grieving, healing and feeling all that this life had in store for me. Poetry for me, is not just a mere collection of words brought together but it is more about undressing of my soul in order to discover the hidden yet the most beautiful parts of my life. This book features the very essence of love and compassion, the very beauty of stars and the moon, the very concept of death and soul, the very demands of the body, both physical and spiritual and most importantly the very fragment of my own heart.

For a moment, forget who you were or who you will be but instead celebrate who you are ,today. With every piece of my writing, I aim at uncovering the hidden you. So, what are you waiting for, let us set on a journey of self dicovery and self love.

LIVE, LAUGH AND LOVE.

With love,

Isha

Chapter1

The cosiest corner of my room,

reminds me of you.

(Come back home love, the corner is still waiting for you)

Chapter2

I wish you could love me,
in the way you wanted me
to love you.
(Maybe you never understood my way)

Chapter3

Let us forget
that we actually
met.
(Let me go away from the pain)

Chapter4

I gave you love,
but
you never returned it.
(Nevermind, I will learn to love my own soul)

Chapter5

I am ready to forget you,
if you are ready to forgive me,
for loving you.
(Why did I commit the sin of loving you?)

Chapter6

The sky is full of stars,
yet none of the stars,
twinkle as bright as your
eyes.
(Your eyes are my stars)

Chapter7

And it is about the hands
that protect you against the
hands that left you
midway.
(Hold such hands tightly)

Chapter8

It was cold
and your warmth
was enough.
(You felt like the cosiest blanket)

Chapter9

Maybe we were meant

to flow in different directions.

(Who knows if one day we would actually meet ?)

Chapter10

Where doubt exists
love finds it difficult
to find its place.
(Because love demands trust)

Chapter11

And then
I love talking to the moon
about my moon.
(You know I love talking to you)

Chapter12

Reminder-
You are allowed to make wrong choices
in order to make the right one.
(Bad experiences are also important)

Chapter13

You deserve a
relationship that
gives you more
reasons to smile
than to cry.
(Because smiling is important)

Chapter14

Your absence made
me learn how
important it is
to value someone's
presence.
(But I know that you will never return)

Chapter15

I can't hold
you forever
but my words
always will.
(My words carry your presence)

Chapter16

To my questions,
he had no answers
but he had the patience to
understand the reason
behind those questions
and this kindness of his
answered all my questions.
(This patience is what I always waited for)

Chapter17

When did I fell in love?
The very moment
you undressed your
soul in front of my
eyes.
(OH! my god, such a beautiful soul)

Chapter18

I crave for the kind
of love strong enough
to value my scars.
(Because scars too deserve love)

Chapter19

If I were to choose
between two
I would choose none
and
if it is really love
then options seem
unreasonable because
it is about celebrating
the one,
your special one.
(And noone can ever replace you)

Chapter20

I wish to make
every capability of
not loving you
incapable.
(Because I really want to love you)

Chapter21

That day while dancing
in the rain
she looked like a
piece of art
I wanted to touch her
but she looked so
beautifully fragile
that I feared breaking
her apart
that day while dancing
in the rain
she looked like a piece of art.
(I just wanted to watch her)

Chapter22

On my low days,
I remember how
you made me feel
good on my low days.
(Those were the days)

Chapter23

Love should not
hurt and
if it is hurting
it is simply not love.
(Stay away from the kind of love that just hurts)

Chapter24

I still can't
speak of love
without spelling
your name.
(Can I call you love, then?)

Chapter25

To let go off
someone quietly
even while carrying
a tempest in the heart
is thus called strength.
(OH! Darling, you are so strong)

Chapter26

And I don't know
whether you felt
the warmth or
was it just cold
was it fire
was it water
or
was it just another hand to hold?
(Tell me, what it was ?)

Chapter27

She was autumn
he came like
spring.
(Brought with him flowers and fragrance)

Chapter28

Good are many
Better are few
but if it is about falling in love
then why the best choice is
always you?
(Why?)

Chapter29

You left me the same day
you asked
"what if I would leave you someday"?
(This question is enough to break my heart)

Chapter30

Darling,
You have done a lot
for others
more than you will ever
realize
but now it is time
to rest
breathe and
appreciate yourself.
(Your love is so special)

Chapter31

For love to be an art
I tried to be the artist.
For pain to be an art
You proved to be the artist.
(You were best at painting a broken heart)

Chapter32

Sometimes
all you need to try
is
hug and cry.
(Those arms feel so good)

Chapter33

A part of
me still wants
to love you.
(But, what about the rest of the parts ?)

Chapter34

People come back to you
when you don't need their back.
People leave you when you
need them to stay.
And then there are people
who stay for seasons
without reasons.
(Different people teach you different lessons)

Chapter35

You deserve every
piece of peace.
(You are truly worthy of it)

Chapter36

And he never brought
me a rose
but to protect me against
every storm
he was always on his toes.
(And this care of his was enough)

Chapter37

I cannot listen
to my favourite
song and not
think of you.
(You are my favourite song)

Chapter38

I want to be
your warm cup of
coffee on the days
you are feeling cold.
(I hope you enjoy your coffee)

Chapter39

Eternal love-
Only I could seize
the moments
I spend with you.
(The only thing I wish to seize)

Chapter40

Genuine people will
never test you
instead they will
even love you
in your darkest times.
(This is why good people are so beautiful)

Chapter41

Cold were the hands
warm was the heart
Amidst the darkness
of the night
you seemed like a
piece of art.
(Such a mesmerizing piece of art)

Chapter42

My eyes had
a sky,
but you failed
to notice the moon,
you failed to
notice you.
(Why were you not able to notice ?)

Chapter43

Love returns in
unexpected ways,
amidst a thunderstorm
you might see some
sun rays.
(Learn to embrace such rays)

Chapter44

Dear self-
It is so strong of
you to smile even
after holding so much
pain in your heart.
You are so brave.
Forget about the world
I an proud of you.
(Dear self, I love you)

Chapter45

Maybe
I was meant to
love more.
(And so I did)

Chapter46

A soulmate would
never promise to you
what he cannot
promise to himself.
(And this is why we call him , " A soulmate ")

Chapter47

You deserve to be
loved in the same
manner in which you love.
(You deserve every kind of love)

Chapter48

You never wanted to
love me and I
couldn't stop loving
you.
(My love knew no complications)

Chapter49

I hope when this
world is so heavy
so much that you start
losing yourself
remember to turn
back to your home
remember to turn
back to me.
(I will be waiting for you)

Chapter50

To the sky of my love
I just needed the stars
and you.
(You complete my sky)

Chapter51

Every morning
I still wait for you with
a cup of tea
the same tea you loved
the same cup you chose
the same amount of sugar you preferred
the same quantity of milk you poured
the same warmth you cherished
everything is same
but what about you.
(Are you still the same?)

Chapter52

I miss how
you brushed your
fingers through
my hair.
(I miss how you held my hand)

Chapter53

I hope you find
someone who loves
you more and hurts
you less.
(Love should not hurt)

Chapter54

You are the piece of
poetry
I took years to write
and
will take a forever
to celebrate.
(My favourite piece of poetry)

Chapter55

Some things become
stronger after breaking,
Heart
for instance.
(Broken but beautiful)

Chapter56

In the noise of chaos
I could hear my
silence screaming.
There were many ears
which could hear
but lesser were the ones
which could comprehend
my silence and my fear.
(To understand silence demands patience)

Chapter57

What is love?
Tugging your companion
inside the cosy blanket and
whispering goodnight in
his ears.
(Another language of love)

Chapter58

If he is meant to
be with you,
he will.
If he isn't
then please stop hurting yourself.
(Please stop waiting for him)

Chapter59

A space in my heart
belongs to love.
A space in my heart
belongs to you.
(That special place)

Chapter60

I hope you
find the exact kind
of love you dream of
every night when
you stare at the moon.
(And I still hope)

Chapter61

This time when
you wrapped your
hands around me,
It felt like a burden
of the guilt behind
not letting you free.
(I am sorry)

Chapter62

To dream of a dream
so beautiful like you
is my reason of dreaming.
(The best reason of dreaming)

Chapter63

And the beauty lies
in your voice and
your choice to call out
the same name
everytime
you are in pain.
(That name has your trust)

Chapter64

Find someone who
finds beauty in you
not just for days
but for years
not just in your smile
but also in your tears.
(Because you are effortlessly beautiful)

Chapter65

Everytime you touch me,
I feel like holding
that touch.
(Such a warm touch)

Chapter66

My pen moves
while it writes about
others.
BUT
My pen dances
while it writes about
you.
(How does my pen know that I love you ?)

Chapter67

My poetries beat for you
I wonder if you will ever feel them.
(Will you ever feel them ?)

Chapter68

I wrote about you
before I met you
because I always knew
that someday I will
surely meet you.
(And I did trust my confidence)

Chapter69

I wish I could
rewrite my destiny
to include your name
in it.
(You are the best part of my destiny)

Chapter70

Every night I tell
the stars about my
moon.
Every night I tell
the stars about
you.
(You are my favourite story to narrate)

Chapter 71

You will heal
but it will
take time.
(Trust the process)

Chapter72

Sunsets
You and
Me.
(Who said magic does not exist?)

Chapter73

Intimacy would be
us gazing at the
moon with your
hands wrapped
around my waist.
(The most intense kind of intimacy)

Chapter74

Fly me to the moon
I want to meet a star
I want to meet him.
(Atleast for once)

Chapter75

I pretend it does not
hurt by seeing you
with someone else
but deep inside it
is tearing me apart.
(And you are not even noticing)

Chapter76

You skipped me
like an unwanted chapter
I read you completely
like an intense story.
My story started with
"You"
continued with
"Us"
and ended with
"Me".
(I thought you were the author
but you were just a character)

Chapter77

I keep on finding you
in my blanket whenever
darkness scares me.
(You are comforting space)

Chapter78

Let's be friends
before becoming lovers.
Lovers, who are
friends at the first place,
prove to be
the true lovers.
(Friendship is important in love)

Chapter79

From loneliness
to serenity.
I found myself
celebrating soltitude.
(Now, soltitude seems beautiful)

Chapter80

I got so little
of you even after
giving so much
of me.
(And I am happy with this little)

Chapter81

Watching you go
away seemed like
watching a fierce thunderstorm
with no roof above my head.
(Such a terrible storm)

Chapter82

Like a dream you
embraced me at night
Like a dream you
left me in the morning
Like a dream
OH!
You were just like
a dream that could
never come true.
(A dream, just a dream)

Chapter83

Maybe one day
I will travel the
world with my world
I will travel
the world with you.
(And I am waiting for that day)

Chapter84

If they are not
worried about
losing you.
(Are they really your people?)

Chapter85

And at last of
everything,
You are left with
memories that
become your
everything.
(Memories last long)

Chapter86

It was that face,
The first time I
saw it I knew,
I wanted to see
the same face for
the rest of my life.
(A face worth remembering)

Chapter87

Every night I
utter your name
before sleeping
to make my dreams
even better.
(And your name makes my night)

Chapter88

Find someone
who sits beside
you when everyone
else leave your side.
(Your special someone)

Chapter89

How sad to
miss someone
who will never
come back.
(How painful it is !)

Chapter90

You are all I ever wanted
and all I could ever need.
(You , just you)

Chapter91

We are all
in search of
our
"happily ever after".
(And, this search is long)

Chapter92

Never forget to
forgive the one
who gave you so
many beautiful
moments to remember.
(Because sometimes it gets too late)

Chapter93

Let me hold
your hand before
you take it away.
Let me hold the
time before it
passes away.
(Let me hold your hand)

Chapter94

Wish to turn back
urge to hold the same hand
is still there.
But is the grip still
strong enough to
secure it.
(Is the strength still there ?)

Chapter95

It takes a moment
to express and a
lifetime to regret.
Pour your heart out
before it stops beating.
(Learn to express)

Chapter96

And at last
we all wish this
world to be less
demanding and
more accepting.
(Acceptance is the key to the door of happiness)

Chapter97

And some stories end
but they leave behind
broken characters that
live forever.
(Stories end but characters live)

Chapter98

From
"You and I"
to
"us".
From
"Trying to trust you"
to
"You becoming the reason
behind my trust".
(You and I)

Chapter99

Under my skin
existed a whole different
world that you
failed to notice.
(Under my skin lies a whole universe)

Chapter100

How long can you love
them wihout them
loving you back?
(For how long ?)

Chapter101

To the home
of my hopes
you proved to
be the comfort.
(So much comfort)

Chapter102

And nobody could
ever hold my hand
in the way he did.
(His touch was special)

Chapter103

Conversing while
stargazing is
another name for
LOVE.
(Stargazing is a language of love)

Chapter104

Baby, you will find someone,
your someone. someday.
(Because,there is a someone for everyone)

Chapter105

More than sympathy,
you deserve empathy.
more than lust,
you deserve trust.
more than a maybe,
you deserve a forever.
more than a love that could last,
you deserve a love that would last.
(More than pain, you deserve love)

Chapter106

To my wounds wide open,
you seemed to act like a bandage.
(You helped me in healing)

Chapter107

Despite my heart noticing
everything you had done
wrong to me,
my heart still
keeps a space reserved for you
to stay.
(I have to learn to stop loving those who hurt me)

Chapter108

My poetries had all that
I felt for you,
but you never intended
to read ,
to understand,
and to feel them.
(I wish someday you will give them a read)

Chapter109

Oh,
I wish you
understood my
kind of love,
my kind love.
(Love demands kindness)

Chapter110

If love is a poetry,
you are surely a
beautiful poet.
(Because you write so well)

Chapter111

When you break a promise,
you also break a heart.
(Promises should not be broken)

Chapter112

Oh!
My heart stuck between
two chapters-
To let go off what hurts
or
To let off who hurts.
(Which chapter will complete my story ?)

Chapter113

It takes a lot of courage to love,
and even more to love again.
(And, you are courageous)

Chapter114

Nothing is so warming than
hugging you after a bad day.
(Your hugs are my fuel)

Chapter115

You do not choose love,

instead

love chooses you.

(And love knows ,when and how to choose)

Chapter116

For one night,
hold me tight
For one night,
let no darkness strike your sight
For one night,
be my moon, be the moonlight
For one night,
let me
hold you tight.
(Just hold me tight)

Chapter117

You are still young, you still have chances to grow.
no matter how dark is the night,
the morning sun will surely be bright.
(Trust the process)

Chapter118

In my empty bed,
I kept on searching for some love.
In my empty bed,
I kept on searching for you.
(My bedsheet still smells of you)

Chapter119

I wish that you understand
that it was not me
who lied but it was
you who was too
afraid to accept the truth.
(How randomly you called me a liar ?)

Chapter120

Maybe,
when the time is bad
you will find me
holding your hand.
(I will never let you suffer alone)

Chapter121

You are a piece of art
carved by my love.
(A beautiful piece of art)

Chapter122

They might hear you,
but that does not mean
that they understand you.
(Are they just listening ?)

Chapter123

Sometimes,
a person proves to be
your home.
(And a home is the best place)

Chapter124

I used to wonder what,
" A fairy tale " felt like
And it is this,
it is us.
(The most beautiful fairy tale)

Chapter125

A shattered heart
too deserves a chance
to love.
(Every heart deserves love)

Chapter126

So,
when was the last time
you laughed your heart out?
(When was the last time you were happy?)

Chapter127

A smile so bright,
it can illuminate the
darkest night.
(Yes, I am talking about your smile.)

Chapter128

I do not mind
taking different roads until
I find the real one.
(Afterall, life is an adventure)

Chapter129

To appreciate a rose
are many,
but to accept the thorns,
are none.
To love the scars,
it requires courage,
and the one who does that
is surely a beautiful one.
(Acceptance is a language of love)

Chapter130

My heart utters the word
" LOVE "
whenever I see you.
(Isn't it enough?)

Chapter131

Even if the world ends up now,
I would love to die in your arms.
(A place worth dying in)

Chapter132

All I wanted from you was
to understand my efforts,
no flowers,
no chocolates,
no gifts.
(Just comprehension)

Chapter133

Every place you kissed me
now feels like a scar hoping
to heal.
(I wish to heal every scar you gave me)

Chapter134

We went from
strangers to lovers.
From the two who knew
nothing about each other,
to the two who know
everything about each other.
(That is how, a love story works)

Chapter135

A part of me died
with that last touch
of yours.
(Your touch was special)

Chapter136

Sometimes my eyes speak
what my words cannot
explain.
(Eyes are so powerful)

Chapter137

And if our love was
a fire,
it would be the only fire
worth burning in.
(The fire of love)

Chapter138

My first morning scenery-
Staring you sleep
with such grace and beauty.
(Such a beautiful scenery)

Chapter139

And it is about the eyes
that search for you
in the crowd.
(Those eyes are worthy of your love)

Chapter140

The limits for my love
for you are limitless.
(My kind of love is diiferent)

Chapter141

"Look at the moon",
she whispered from her fragile lips.
"I am looking at it",
he said while looking in her eyes.
(She was his moon)

Chapter142

Tired of fighting,
she chose to take a break.
Tired of loving people too much,
she chose to give them a break.
(A lesson that she learned a really hard way)

Chapter143

And at times,
I crave the taste of you.
(I still crave for you)

Chapter144

I might be a poet
but you will
always be my poetry.
(A poetry, I will never be tired of reading)

Chapter145

And when in dark,
You held my hand.
To know if I was feeling safe,
I realised how bright our future will be.
(A bright future)

Chapter146

The word
"love"
was made so that we could find each other.
(And then I found you)

Chapter147

And when the stars argued
that their moon is better.
I asked them if they have
ever met my moon,
I asked them if they have
ever met you.
(Why is my moon the best ?)

Chapter148

Strange,
how beautifully we hide pain.
(And still manage to smile)

Chapter149

Giving time to someone,

and wasting time on someone

are two different things.

(And to understand the difference between the two is so important)

Chapter150

To sit beside you,
and talk about nothing yet everything,
is more soothing than anything else.
(With you even nothing seems everything)

Chapter151

Seven billion people
in the world yet
I only wish to be
with you every moment.
(Why are you so beautiful ?)

Chapter152

And then,
sometimes
the people who loved us the most
tend to
hurt us the most.
(Life is a strange game)

Chapter153

Stay away from the people
who only know how
to bless the rose and
curse the thorns.
(What is a rose without few thorns ?)

Chapter154

Give yourself the love
you never received.
(After all, self love is so important)

Chapter155

We might meet again,
someday
maybe in dreams.
(A dream worth cherishing)

Chapter156

And I lay awake at nights
thinking of the nights
we spent together.
(Dear nights, why were you so comforting?)

Chapter157

I was never a night person,
until the moon began to
sing his name.
(All night long, I kept on listening to the moon)

Chapter158

In your
silence,
I found
my answers.
(And then no words were needed)

Chapter159

Silence only
hurts when
I think of
your voice.
(I can even hear when you murmur my name)

Chapter160

You are my
favourite place
to kiss.
(Such a soft place, indeed)

Chapter161

Don't tell my
dreams I am
chasing them.
Let me give them
a surprise.
(Dear dreams, I am coming)

Chapter162

If you were a flower,
I would be longing
to be a butterfly.
(You are the most beautiful flower)

Chapter163

Take me back to
those times where
we didn't have to
pretend to love each other.
(To pretend is to deceive)

Chapter164

I do not fear being alone,
I just fear being without you.
(Without you, even spring feels like autumn)

Chapter165

To cry is to
not become weak
or helpless.
To cry is to
let go off the pain
to help yourself heal.
And remember,
healing is not possible
without grieving.
(Dear tears, thankyou for helping me heal)

Chapter166

We tend to forget
less when we get more.
But it is important
to value less,
because it is
important to remember
that less came as more
when you had nothing.
(Then comes the art of contentment)

Chapter167

It is not about

you, me and

the world.

But

It is about

you, me and

love.

(And my love matters more than the world)

Chapter168

I think of
my moon
while watching
the moon.
I think of
you while
watching
the moon.
(And it is about the moon and my moon)

I hope that I was able to touch atleast a part of your heart. I am glad that you actually made through the entire journey of living different yet beautiful emotions. Nothing can make me happier else than your love and support.

I would love to be your bestfriend, hear from you, the undiscovered stories of your life. Feel free to reach out to me.

Your reviews are my fuel. And if you liked my work, do not forget to share your thoughts on my book either on the official website of notionpress and amazon or you can directly contact me on instagram.

My instagram handle is as follows-

@notalwaysisha

Eagerly waiting to hear from you guys.

Love,

Isha